Four Seasons in the Sierra

Four Seasons in the Sierra

By Jillian Makoutz

Art by Claire Lawrenson
Book design by Erin Rufledt Hunter

GRASS AND SKY PRESS
grassandskypress@gmail.com

ISBN: 979-8-218-26475-8

This book is dedicated to anyone who has accompanied me into the Sierra Mountains.

"If you have ever gone to the woods with me, I must love you very much." - Mary Oliver

Contents

Spring

Go to the Fields 3
Snowplant 4
Communion with Fear 5
Viola Sheltonii 8
Sun Come Lately 9
Tasiyagnunpa 10
Redwings 12
Snowmelt 13
Elderflowers 14

Summer

Electric 17
Lady Night 18
Hexagenia 19
Last Rays 20
Great Blue Heron 21
Lakes Basin 23
Bittern 25
Snake Charmer 26
Sometimes at the Bird Preserve 27

Autumn

Red Sorrel 31
Nuthatch 32
First Frost 33
Afterglow 34
Aspens 35
Cattails 36
Instant Autumn 37
Moonrise 39

WINTER

Worlds Apart 43
Sudden Sunset 44
Winter Night 45
All the World's Oceans 46
Bird Leaves 47
Waiting Before Sunrise 48
Outside Everywhere 49
Water Ouzel 50

Spring

Go to the Fields

You will never see a meadowlark
At the feeder

For this particular honor
You must go to the fields

Bring kindhearted friends
Full of yearning and curiosity

It doesn't seem to matter how late spring arrives
(Though to be specific, the third week of March
Should do nicely)

Wait
Wait in silence
You may hear the watery trill
The yearning
The curiosity
And wonder if you are overhearing your friends

Indeed it is the voice of one
Who would gladly make your acquaintance
From a safe distance
If you are gentle and considerate
And not plowing the field
Where it has made its nest

Perhaps you will behold it perched on a fence
With grace
Determination
And that brave yellow throat

But even if you've never
Heard a meadowlark in your life
Go to the fields
Alone or in good company
Sing a song out into the world

Snowplant

What is this bright spot
On the forest floor
Of a wasted winter
Where snow still lingers
Under the shadows of the trees
And the wind still whispers
In currents of cold

What electric, neon,
Hot pink globe of iridescent
Flame
Is emerging into this world of faded,
Used to,
And gray?

Perhaps you thought, like me,
That this winter would last forever
And color would never come again
To the world inside and outside of you

But here we find
A snowplant
Unfurling its perfect self
In an intricate
Kaleidoscope pattern
Inflorescent
Incomprehensible

Incomprehensible that such a color
Should exist in nature

Raceme not fading
As it emerges
Blossoms
Radiates
A beacon of the coming spring

Communion with Fear

*We reached the old wolf in time to watch a fierce green fire dying in
her eyes. I realized then and have known ever since that there was
something new to me in those eyes, something known only to her and
to the mountain. -Aldo Leopold*

Her sleek and terrible body
Glided over the fence
Like an animated shadow
Smooth
Supernatural

As I approached
I didn't know what
I expected to see
Nothing?
Perhaps

Her surprise was mild
Compared to mine
That great round face
Body tremendous
Powerful

Healthy
And very much alive

(Three times the size of a coyote,
I thought later when I saw one
Tripping through the sage brush
Ears as big as anything)

And face to face now
With the coyote's grand and majestic cousin

I had a passing childhood memory
Of the recurring kind
A nightmare where she would chase me

Sometimes I would fall
And feel her strong legs

Rush over my back

This dream came back to me
In full color
(Or black and white
As the old debate goes)

I stared now into eyes
That were
Surprisingly
Staring right back at me

Provokingly tauntingly
With a hint of
Dare I say it?
Playfulness

Had I not been in my car
I fear we would have started the dance
All over again
The chasing
The running
The dream come to life

For this animal was not afraid

I drive by the spot
I saw her
Most days now
I can't help but fare her well
Wherever she fares

I imagine the masterpiece
Of her body
Shot down
By anger
Fear

Fear of her
Who is not afraid
Fear of her
Who does not see her own existence as a problem

A tremor runs through me
An overwhelming feeling
Of protection
And awe

Homage is my lasting testament
To this commune
With the lone wolf of Loyalton
May she find what she is looking for

Viola Sheltonii

The ground
Becomes soft
Saturated

Below brown pine needles
Rocks
And the shells and seed pods of last autumn

This landscape once seeming barren
Is beginning a new task
Of waterleaf peeking

And here is where Shelton's violet
Has returned
Quietly

Its leaves are
Perfect
Dark green, and fine, like lace

As if the leaves weren't a gift enough,
The blossoms are open and
Facing up to the sky

So bright
And all-yellow truthful
That it really did happen again

The impossible, unfurling so quietly,
So quickly and hopefully
We are already here, on the other side of this change

(Published in Tiny Seeds Literary Journal, 7/2/23)

Sun Come Lately

A ray of sun glances
Whimsical
Upon the expectant land

As if by some happy mistake
A shaft of sky opens
And suddenly everything is

Ablaze
In the warm embrace
Of someone come lately

Illuminating
Transforming
Momentarily lucid

Waiting at hand is the cold and gray
Dormant
Forgotten

In this shallow embrace
Sublime meeting
Of a fairweather friend

Tasiyagnunpa
(The Yellow Lark that Speaks Lakota)

The snow melts
The fields clear out
Wake up
Mellow
Brighten

And now the long awaited time
Has come again
Morning after morning
I anticipate
Any day now

Until surely
One day a call
Clear as anything
Cuts through the fields and roads

As if the very grass
At my feet has burst into song
And will I ever hear it
Singing, calling, questioning again?

Yes! Here it is again!
And if every flower in every field
Had hopped up onto the fencepost
And belted out its praises to the sky

I wouldn't be surprised

Meadowlarks speak Lakota
And if a Tribal Elder was present
They would understand something
I only feel with my heart

For it seems that all of the glory
And grace of the fields
(the streams, too) have come together
In one curious, triumphant call

Here I am!
Are you glad I'm here?
I'm glad! (laughing)
I am so glad to be back home!

*(Dedicated to Vic Runnels and published with acceptance
from Bunny Sings Wolf of the Lakota tribe)*

Redwings

Throaty proclamation
As of mud
And sudden creeks gurgling
A rekindling host
To roadside rambles
And marshy glades
This the great announcement
To life exultant
From the dead, white and gray
To the rain soaked, reedy floods of spring
The red-winged blackbirds
Have returned

Snow Melt

Blue water flows
Under icy crags
Cold the cliff's
Snowmelt
Of early spring

April around the
Corner
The first new month
Born of moss
And daffodil

Ice giving way now
To saturated loam
Spongy, absorbent
Sprouting in blossoms
Of green stars

As if the earth
Has softened now
To embrace us all
In the bosom
Of her heart

Forgetting the long,
Cold separation
The hostility of wind
And the terror of snow
In drifts unfathomable

This welcoming back
Out of doors
Into sunlit green
And the yearning songs
Of birds and frogs

This sweet return
Like the remembrance
Of an old and dear friend
Has melted and washed
Everything anew

Elderflowers

We travel the dusty road
Past manzanita and bitterbrush
A creek softly gurgling nearby

Searching for the white crowns
Like lace foaming on the ends of
Fingerlike branches

Elder, eldest
She's an old woman with her hair of white
And yet her face as young as the dawn

The floral scent is sticky
Somehow pungent and savory
Each flower a tiny, perfect star

Here on the mountainside
She reigns over everything thorny
And thick in the sagey underbrush

We could wait until the dusty blue berries
Ripen in clusters, lucious as grapes
The sharp scent still reminiscent of her blossoms

But we are here now, in this moment
With the bees and the sunshine
Ready to bottle up spring

Ready to harvest a few soft, white clusters
Pollen-dusted and delicate
Afterwards, we soak our feet in the cold, rushing water nearby

We rinse our faces, laughing and singing
Amongst the Sierra Rein Orchids
And Horsetails

Tonight we will bottle up spring
In all of her golden, syrupy brightness
Save it to pull out at a future time
When we are in need of her wisdom and strength

Summer

Electric

Brightly the golden fields switch on
While the mountains remain obscured
By the thick, cobalt canvas
Of a coming storm

A storm that has thrown shadows
And light askew
Scattered in layers
And sheets of wind and rain

The viscous air lurches
And everywhere in sudden movement
The birds are reeling
In nervous or joyful flight

Slap! Come the heavy, precious
Drops from above
On everything alike
And could it ever be enough?

For a moment the aquarian sky
Heaves and lets go
Releasing
Bearing water to the earth

This violent disturbance of atmosphere moves
Tearing, cracking
The distance darkened
Too soon away

Yet lingering in the dampened fields
Is the aroma of every flower
Every plant
Every molecule of sage

Awakened, renewed
Lifting their sweet
Rain-drenched offerings
In redolent gratitude

Lady Night

Lady night
Cover us in the
Thickness of your blankets
Smooth
Soothe

The dark lace
Hem of your garment
Transparent
Entices a celestial view
Of eternal and ethereal orbs

Your heartbeat is an earthy
And winged
Rhythm
Croaking humming buzzing creeping
Along with the sonorous pulse of an owl

Our bodies
Warm and brave
Are hiding under your dense thicket
Of branches and bracken
In search of deeper rivers and streams

Moonlit
We peer into this vast world
World of stinging biting preying stalking
Wild wildness
Under the sleepy gaze of your tangled eyelashes

Cover us
In your long, black
Elysian veil

(Some of us will make it
Tonight
Some of us will survive)

Hexagenia

In the grinding out of time
On wheels fixed with iron and stone
Age upon age
The strong
Survive
Yet a thread weaved into the tapestry
(silver and lisle)
An ephemeral host
Emerges
Glistening
In translucent life
Increasing in numbers
Teeming, throbbing
The fragile wanderers
The daytrippers
In great numbers arrive
Undaunted by the wind
Or the sometimes breeze of June
In clouds unmatched
They shed their jeweled skin
In a summer fever
And knit their way to the sky
In the fervor and pleasure of a one night stand
And this is it
Defying all odds
In the constant hum of age upon age
The survival of the weak

Last Rays

Once the last rays disappeared
Behind the mountains
Everything changed
The meadow, blue and calm now
Let out a sigh
No longer illuminated by
The intense, unswerving gaze
Of the sun

I could watch the grass
Continue forever
Swaying like the
Up and down
Cadence of the sea
Each head lifted
In the possibility of seed
And then bowed in reverence and relief

The air swirling with the kinetic
Diving of insects
The light changing each minute
On the face of the mountains
And the earth
Letting out a cool
And serene
Dewy breath of dusk

Great Blue Heron

We had been aware of his presence for several days
Hanging around between the creek
And the road
Hunting and gathering, one would presume

The road

Sometimes the road was like a paved strip
Of earth, barely distinguishable
From the fields
The forest

Until, with unexpected force
Like a blade sharpening itself on stone
Like a sudden tornado
It was devastating

(I don't know where they come from
Driving like hell through the night)

Even the puca, on its reckless steed
Has standards
Has rules

And this wasn't an ushering in of fall
This was high summer
The time of joy

We found him in the morning
A patch on each shoulder
The color of rust

I never knew that
About the Great Blue Heron
I never knew just how colorful he was

And how tall
Still pointing like an arrow
In his death

His taut body ready to spring
Into the shallow waters
Bringing back his fish
His beak a spear
His legs curled so delicately
Yet contorted in instant pain

Dead at the scene

What will we do now
Without you in our lives
Gracing us with your calm and
Stable presence

The world lost something
Magnificent that July night
To the sometimes reckless joining
Of wheel to road

You are gone forever
And yet we will
Look for you
Desperately
In those you've left behind

(In Honor of Kevin Walsh)

Lakes Basin

Late in the afternoon
Forsaking the swelter
Of a dry, hot day

We pack provisions,
Towels, sweaters,
A thermos of tea

We arrive at the lake before sunset
And watch the people,
Dogs, radios and rafts leave

We quickly pick up abandoned
Flip flops
Gum wrappers

Plastic dental flossers,
Pool toys,
We make a pile, we throw away

The lake is ours now
We drift in and out
Of cold water

Watching the faces of the mountains
Change from yellow
To rose

The silence of a single
Osprey
Our only companion

The final rays of the sun
Linger on the frosted peaks
Where last winter's snow still clings

Perhaps no one ever told you
The world could be so perfect
And serene

They never told me
I had to find it
At a mountain lake

In high summer
When everyone else had gone home
To escape the silence and the cold

Bittern

The grasses bend, quiver
In an expanse of green and sudden brown
For the bittern is there amongst them
Beak upward
Yet curved slightly
In a smile

> With the reeds
> Among the reeds
> One of the reeds

Swaying swaying
Body more pliable than its call
Which is clear and yet mingling
So well in the
Sora sandhill snipe chorus
Of a summer afternoon

Deeper is the drum
Stone dropping into a well
Gurgle and thump
Of the bittern

A constant cadence
Sounding as if to say

> I am returned
> Not just to the water
> But to myself
> Who is of the water

(Published in Tiny Seeds Literary Journal, 11/24/2023)

Snake Charmer

When I found her
On the trail up ahead
She was holding a snake

Not just holding it
But talking to it
While its tongue flickered like a candle flame

Its eyes cool and serene

Its body smooth as stone

Its tail uncoiled and hanging
Relaxed around her arm

Who is this that sees a snake
Hidden and moving
Silently under her feet

And thinks to pick it up
And become better acquainted

I've seen her live her life this way
Picking us all up
Holding us
And becoming better acquainted

In her is the knowing
In us the being known

Snake charmer
Friend of the wild

Sometimes at the Bird Preserve

Sometimes the days smooth out
And the lines I've forgotten
The ones on the horizon I know all too well
Come back to greet me in pastel
And remind me of something deep and simple

I am home in this world for just a time
And that time is now

Nothing has changed with my hands or my feet
To alienate me just yet
Familiar faces surround me
And the things I've loved to do in this life
Are still right in front of me to do

Hold those hands
Run with the feet that will join
To prospects unknown
For darkness is ahead
And there is no way back

But now is the sunset and the muted bird sounds of August
Now is laughter and dancing and the profanity of young boys
still too innocent to really be vulgar

Now is wine with my love and sublime conversation with a world
outside of my world
One turned woman in front of my eyes
A whole expanse of wisdom and youth called daughter

I gather a bouquet of important flowers
I stake my claim to this corner of the planet
By watching a night heron fly home and calling him by name
I say *hello* and *goodbye*, again, to this green earth
And *I hope to see you again soon*

Autumn

Red Sorrel

In the middle of the valley, the cold rain of last night
Has washed everything and gone away
Leaving a few drifting clouds to obscure
The rise and fall of mountain terrain

The panoramic view
Borders on monochromatic
Peaks appear taller, more grand somehow
And everything feels like an exhale

As if to say
We can let go now
We are no longer surviving
The heat and scorch of summer

In this light, which is no longer direct
And white hot
But diffused, mellowed,
The plant life takes on a different hue

The sharp wind is a breath of relief
The sun is angled southward
And the red sorrel is exquisite against this gold grass
And sage green backdrop

Nuthatch

Upside down nuthatch
In glimpses
I catch your bright face and throat
Like a small man freshly shaven
And sporting a warm cloak

You keep your cape tight
Around your shoulders
On this chilly morning
The sun, a thought on the horizon
The clear sky cold, honest

You move with speed and ease
From tree to tree
Up and down and all around
So that I barely see you
Before you are gone again

I know I have heard your call
From the trees
But you are silent
at your trunk work
Like a pale faced shadow

And how is it for you
Little nuthatch
When you are foraging
Is there an up and a down
Or is the entirety of the tree an open plane
By which you excavate at will

First Frost

I have never seen
So many cranes in one place before

As on this sunset-dipped evening
After the first frost

The cold is still deep
Cutting through the sun warmth

Reminding me that the hospitality of the land
Lies far behind now

Darkness will soon be stretching its arm
Over the lines and curves of the valley

Drawing me to my hearth
More often in the coming days

Here the memories must glow now
In the faces of loved ones reminiscing of summer's joy

I watch the colors fade
And the shadows rise on the mountains

Along with the moon
Its blue light ghostly, other worldly

A chill weaves its way
Through the canyon and into my bones

As if the earth was no longer made for any of us
Indoors a certain refuge

The cranes are trilling their fabled goodbyes
Not leaving so much as returning to their far away home

Afterglow

Green fades into sudden gray
Sturdy life withers
Wilts and dries
Into skeletal shadows

The joys we embraced
With the surprise of spring
Have run their course
Their time has come and gone

Yet every colorless thing that remains
In this golden time of year
Is gilded
Embossed in sticky sunlight

We have weathered the first frost
And now the reflection
In our footprints
Shines

Some things are only
Heightened
And sweetened
By low temperatures

Let it be so with our own cold souls
May we find the bright times brighter
In the sugared sunset of this
Afterglow

Aspens

Autumn is unfolding
And up through the canyon we go

The hills are blushing
In sparse patches

Of burnt red and
Rabbit brush yellow

Like so many holy-rolling
Burning bush willows

Up the mountainside the sky is blue
Cloudless

The cliffs are manzanita green
And dead-branch gray

Behold
This temporary glowing

Of ruby and saffron coins
Where the creek runs cold

The aspens are ablaze
Like dancing embers

Caught by the sun
Each leaf luminous

Laughing
Celebrating

A secret world on fire

Cattails

All of nature has softened out now
Into the static fluff of the cattails
Lighter than the breeze
Now gentle after days of turbulent, raging storm

The heavy velvet heads
Rock and sway
Showing their fleecy undergarments
Where the downy seeds have burst at the seams

My children find their brown fur
Too irresistible to refuse
Their hands eagerly working into the softness
Underneath

Creamy white clouds burst forth
In a celebration of possibility and life
Ecstatic is the young person
That discovers this simple pleasure

To release the cattails into the breeze
Into the wild
With the hope
That next year there will be more

The seed heads once so tight and contained
Come free, expanding
Until the wooly cloud
Grows to be twice the size

And what is growth, anyways
If not the dying in the fall
That brings through the darker days ahead
The hope of a fuller and more bountiful spring

Instant Autumn

It is becoming
I turn my head and here
It is again
The sudden transformation
The quiet changer has worked
An instant evolution of green to gold
And blaze of red

Nature is radiant

The dusty pine needle paths
Drenched in the smell of sap
Are glorious for a ramble
Now that the earth has turned
Further away from the scorching summer

Warmth still rises up from the trail
And the way the light refracts
Through golden aspen coins and alder
Makes everything feel somehow
Closer

Perhaps nature is huddling in
For a last embrace
Before leaving off for the winter
And this is her goodbye party

If so she is well dressed indeed
In her finest and richest tapestries
Bejeweled with rosehips and berries
Crowned with aster and gilded leaves

The sweetest and most bitter
Of farewell parties
Is this grand departure...
Leaving so soon?

Yet the deep thrill that is in everything out of doors
Is electrifying
I listen to its pulse

Asking to mirror this motley phenomenon

Change me, too

Moonrise

My belly swells
(There is a glow
Over that crook in the mountains)
We walk on
The light inching towards us

I feel movement inside
(The mountains emanating
Such light)
Heavy steps, but energy
To continue forward

Full belly, full moon
(She is rising over the mountains now
Every tree a clear silhouette)
She is rising
Crowning
The intensity
The searing inhale exhale
Entrance and exit

A new something
A leaving behind
This transformation is
All consuming
We look around
And nothing is the same
The moon is drenching everything
Now
In light

Winter

Worlds Apart

There is a low mist
Hanging over Downieville
This morning

Pine mountains to the
East
Are dusted in white

Each spire standing out
In delicate frost covered
Detail

I can follow the snowline with my eyes
Until it changes to dark green
And low fog

Down to the river
Which gurgles happily
Untouched by winter's cold

Last night the flakes fell in torrents
Preventing my love from
Returning over the pass

Here I look out on fog drenched trees
A chorus of rushing water
And ouzel serenades

On the other side of the mountain
He is waking to a silence
Of snow drifts and complication

An hour away
And worlds apart
Let us hope it isn't always so

(For Joshua)

43

Sudden Sunset

In a sudden sunset forest
In a certain glow of light
The last rays of day
Cast their colorful fire

We watch the deepening
The layers of orange upon orange
The tapestry of trees
Weaving in and out of the

Momentary bright

And if only I could capture this vast ember
Into my palm and with pursed lips
Blow on the coal of the sun
And beg it to remain

Here
Cleft in my hand like some forgotten memory
A vibrant seed
Of beauty neverending

(Published in Tiny Seeds Literary Journal, 6/7/2022)

Winter Night

I've only seen your garden
By night
And how the shadows
Dimly hide your face
When you speak of your plans

Plans that expand
Like children playing
Wild and fanciful

Here there is an empty planter
And wall where roses will climb

For now they stand like faint relics
Ghosts of a former existence
That lived and died
Lived and died

I can smell mud soon foaming
Underneath the snow
Baking in the sun

And here there will be worms
Moving and pushing
Underneath your dreams of green

I can see these plans
You are forming on the cold nights
Under the stars
As your breath mixes
with the chill air

I can see that, too.

Life is yours,
My friend
It is all around you now
Underneath your feet
Biding its time
Waiting to stretch itself out to you
Bursting at last, when you least expect it

All the World's Oceans

In the white muffled
Shock gathering
On a certain morning
When stillness and crystals forming
Cling like blankets and sugar spun

When the dripping is gone,
The fair and bright,
And in the air is the clean and distinct
Smell of all the oceans everywhere
Coming to collect in flakes of snow
Gathering from the farthest corners of water
Air
Dust
Rushing upon us in a swirling
Metronome of frosty waves

Here in my cold and vibrant heart
I can almost hear the roar
Taste the churning brine in the air
The moving force that sends me on my way

Anything far away is
Possible
Any distant point can come in
So sudden
That one look
Like the feathered fall of white
Reveals instant change
(Now coming down in sheets
Feet by the hour)

This is how the Sierra goes coastal
How the wildness of the sea
Engulfs us
The torrents of snow are everywhere now,
Racing over the mountains
Pouring from the skies
Making themselves at home
In piles and drifts unfathomable

Bird Leaves

Leaves
Like paralyzed birds
Flutter
Surrendered in the breeze
Lost in a game of tag
One to another
They float
Alive in the air
Like old friends at play
Flying into drifts of snow
Fragmenting
Settling
Only to rise again
In the fright of
Approaching wind prey
Ensnared
Directionless
They dive in ways incomprehensible
Eventually sinking
Freezing thawing decomposing
Becoming one with the soil

Waiting Before Sunrise

One soft trill resounds
Before sunrise
While a surrounding peace
Still rests on the woods
Encased in icy quiet

From a nearby tree
'Oing
A gong reverberates
From a small
And lusty breast

The note echoes
And corkscrews through the air
From bare branch to bare branch
Finally landing
At my ear where I wait
To answer its frolicsome question

Only to hear it again
In feathered mockery
Of the morning
Or delight

Perhaps it knows something
I don't
About the slight lengthening of days
And this subtle, early light

In the frosty stillness
I listen
Scarcely breathing
Afraid of hearing it change its tune

Outside Everywhere

Heavy the fall of water crystalized
Fractalized
Spirographing through the air

Snowflakes flutter into the woods beyond
Deep into the ravine

I pretend I hear them drop
I must go further in
Explore this primordial something

Under an evergreen
I take cover enough to see them
Parachuting an escape from the sky

This morning is an insular capsule of white
Of blanket below and ever shedding blanket
Above

Outside everywhere
Sounds compress
Muffled in the soft gathering

Soon all will be unrecognizable
From this sudden and irretrievable
Incident

Water Ouzel

Water moves
In and out of ice covered cataracts

Gurgling and drumming
Where all else is the solitude of snow

The sun peeks in and out
Through bare-branched, steep-cliff falls

And from the torrent
A black shadow flutters

Rests, dips,
Eddies and dives

Rising again, like a slate colored leaf
The air lifting it from the swells

In the rushing falls there is constant movement
And the water ouzel is at the heart of it

Here it bends and lifts
Its call cutting through the roaring cascades

Like the voice of a thousand waterfalls
Laughing, trilling, at home in the fray

Its tones so playfully clear and full of joy
"Isn't this world a lovely place?"